FOR _____

FROM _____

DATE _____

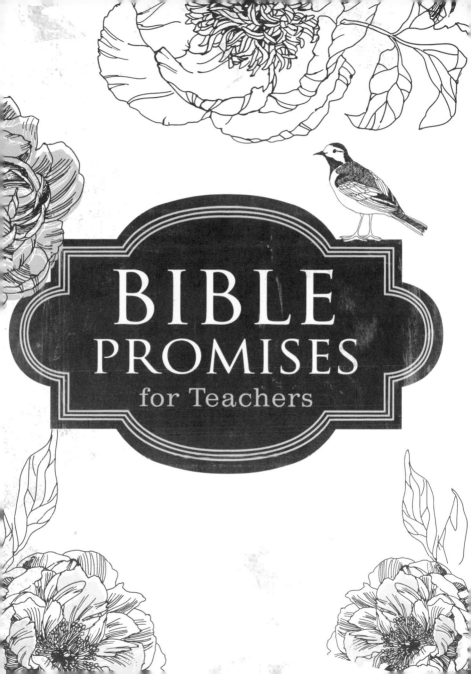

BIBLE
PROMISES
for Teachers

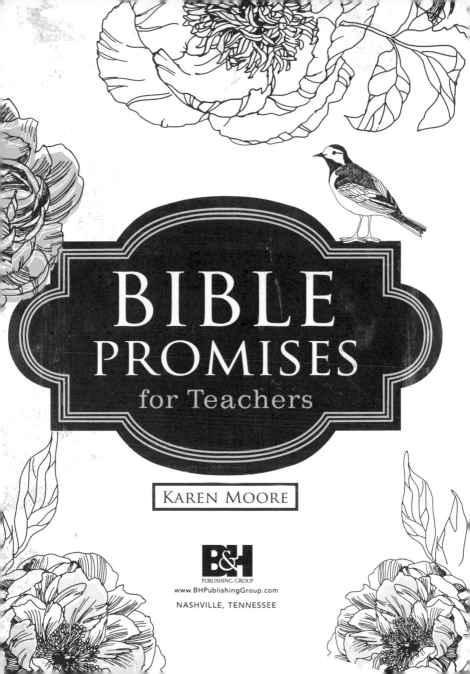

BIBLE PROMISES
for Teachers

KAREN MOORE

B&H
PUBLISHING GROUP
www.BHPublishingGroup.com

NASHVILLE, TENNESSEE

CONTENTS

Introduction \ 1

Chapter 1: Follow the Master Teacher \ 3

Chapter 2: Let God Be Your Guide \ 15

Chapter 3: Lead by Truth and Example \ 26

Chapter 4: Get to Know All Your Students \ 35

Chapter 5: Affirm and Encourage Your Students \ 47

Chapter 6: Guide with Grace and Prayer \ 57

Chapter 7: Demonstrate the Results You Want \ 70

Chapter 8: Take Care of Yourself \ 80

Chapter 9: Love Every Moment \ 91

Chapter 10: Build the Future \ 102

INTRODUCTION

Henry B. Adams said, "A teacher affects eternity; he can never tell, where his influence stops."

Certainly, it was the intention of Jesus to affect eternity. His words and influence changed lives in ways that few of us can fully understand. Yet, He was able to cause transformation by accepting people right where they were and loving them into the kingdom.

As a teacher, you have a similar opportunity. You are surrounded by students who come to you poised to learn, whether they know they need to learn or not, coming to you just as they are, needing acceptance and affirmation.

You are in a position of influence and you help to mold and shape the future.

Your position is not one that God takes lightly. He seeks the best from you as you guide those He entrusts to your care. You're His light, for some, the only light they will come to know and so He offers you strength, assurance, and helpful hints to keep in mind as you teach.

This book uses Scripture to reflect some of the ways Jesus demonstrated ideas and object lessons, how He built followers with love and by being a godly example. You'll see the promise God offers to be near, close by to encourage your work and lighten your load. You are a blessing to others and this book is designed to bless you as you inspire, teach, and lead.

Know that your work is important to each student who crosses your path and to God who created you for His divine purpose. You have no way of knowing how your influence affects eternity.

May God bless you abundantly.

Karen Moore

Chapter 1

FOLLOW THE
MASTER TEACHER

"Follow me, and I will make you fishers of men," Jesus told the weary men who had not caught a thing that day.

What an invitation! A fisherman was supposed to catch fish, supposed to feed others by what he brought in, supposed to make a living by casting a wide net. It sounds like a good description for a teacher, doesn't it? Isn't that the work of someone who casts a vision, a net of possibility, a hope for tomorrow? You are the one who fishes your students out of the place they were and casts them into tomorrow. You are the one who helps them to see that there is more to life than what they might see now. You cause them to try again when they are weary of trying.

Jesus taught men of His day, and He still teaches any of us who are willing to listen and follow His example. He teaches us that there is more, that possibility is always ours because we serve the God of what is possible and not what appears in the present.

Your students need a master teacher. They need someone to look up to, to ask questions of, and to stretch them to become more. As you follow the wisdom and light of Jesus, you bring them closer to all that He would have them be.

Keep casting your net for there is much work to be done.

The Bible Promises . . .

God Teaches the Right Way

> Listen and hear my voice. Pay attention
> and hear what I say. Does the plowman
> plow every day to plant seed? Does he
> continuously break up and cultivate the
> soil? When he has leveled its surface,
> does he not then scatter black cumin and

sow cumin? He plants wheat in rows and
barley in plots, with spelt as their border.
His God teaches him order; He instructs
him. ~ Isaiah 28:23–26

Listen

This is My beloved Son; listen to Him!
~ Mark 9:7

Teach God's Ways

Instruct them about the statutes and
laws, and teach them the way to live and
what they must do. ~ Exodus 18:20

*Give a man a fish and he will eat for a day; teach him
how to fish and he will eat forever. ~ Author Unknown*

Sharing God's Voice

Jesus answered them, "My teaching isn't
Mine but is from the One who sent Me."
~John 7:16

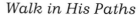

Walk in His Paths

And many peoples will come and say,
"Come, let us go up to the mountain of
the Lord, to the house of the God of
Jacob. He will teach us about His ways
so that we may walk in His paths." For
instruction will go out of Zion and the
word of the Lord from Jerusalem.
~ Isaiah 2:3

Do Not Be Deceived

Therefore, as you have received Christ
Jesus the Lord, walk in Him, rooted and
built up in Him and established in the
faith, just as you were taught, overflow-
ing with gratitude.

Be careful that no one takes you
captive through philosophy and empty
deceit based on human tradition, based
on the elemental forces of the world, and
not based on Christ. ~ Colossians 2:6–8

Teach Me, O Lord!

Teach me Your way, Yahweh, and I will live by Your truth. Give me an undivided mind to fear Your name. ~ Psalm 86:11

I never teach my pupils. I only attempt to provide the conditions in which they can learn. ~Albert Einstein

---

Defining Wisdom

"I will show you what someone is like who comes to Me, hears My words, and acts on them: He is like a man building a house, who dug deep and laid the foundation on the rock. When the flood came, the river crashed against that house and couldn't shake it, because it was well built. But the one who hears and does not act is like a man who built a house on the ground without a foundation. The river crashed against it, and immediately it collapsed. And the destruction of that house was great!" ~ Luke 6:47–49

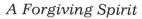

A Forgiving Spirit

"A creditor had two debtors. One owed 500 denarii, and the other 50. Since they could not pay it back, he graciously forgave them both. So, which of them will love him more?"

Simon answered, "I suppose the one he forgave more."

"You have judged correctly," He told him. Turning to the woman, He said to Simon, "Do you see this woman? I entered your house; you gave Me no water for My feet, but she, with her tears, has washed My feet and wiped them with her hair. You gave Me no kiss, but she hasn't stopped kissing My feet since I came in. You didn't anoint My head with olive oil, but she has anointed My feet with fragrant oil. Therefore I tell you, her many sins have been forgiven; that's why she loved much. But the one who is forgiven little, loves little." ~ Luke 7:41–47

Knowing What Is Important

Then He told them a parable: "A rich man's land was very productive. He thought to himself, 'What should I do, since I don't have anywhere to store my crops? I will do this,' he said. 'I'll tear down my barns and build bigger ones and store all my grain and my goods there. Then I'll say to myself, "You have many goods stored up for many years. Take it easy; eat, drink, and enjoy yourself."'

"But God said to him, 'You fool! This very night your life is demanded of you. And the things you have prepared— whose will they be?'

"That's how it is with the one who stores up treasure for himself and is not rich toward God." ~ Luke 12:16–21

Giving Time to Bear Fruit

And He told this parable: "A man had a fig tree that was planted in his vineyard. He came looking for fruit on it and found none. He told the vineyard worker, 'Listen, for three years I have come looking for fruit on this fig tree and haven't found any. Cut it down! Why should it even waste the soil?'

"But he replied to him, 'Sir, leave it this year also, until I dig around it and fertilize it. Perhaps it will bear fruit next year, but if not, you can cut it down.'"
~ Luke 13:6–9

The mediocre teacher tells. The good teacher explains. The superior teacher demonstrates. The great teacher inspires. ~ William A. Ward

Pearls of Wisdom

"Again, the kingdom of heaven is like a merchant in search of fine pearls. When he found one priceless pearl, he went and sold everything he had, and bought it."
~ Matthew 13:45–46

The Role of Humility

He also told this parable to some who trusted in themselves that they were righteous and looked down on everyone else: "Two men went up to the temple complex to pray, one a Pharisee and the other a tax collector. The Pharisee took his stand and was praying like this: 'God, I thank You that I'm not like other people—greedy, unrighteous, adulterers, or even like this tax collector. I fast twice a week; I give a tenth of everything I get.'

"But the tax collector, standing far off, would not even raise his eyes to heaven but kept striking his chest and saying, 'God, turn Your wrath from me—a sinner!' I tell you, this one went down to his house justified rather than the other; because everyone who exalts himself will be humbled, but the one who humbles himself will be exalted."
~ Luke 18:9–14

A Good Word

A word spoken at the right time is like gold apples on a silver tray. ~ Proverbs 25:11

No Worries

"Consider the ravens: They don't sow or reap; they don't have a storeroom or a barn; yet God feeds them. Aren't you worth much more than the birds? Can any of you add a cubit to his height by worrying? If then you're not able to do even a little thing, why worry about the rest?

"Consider how the wildflowers grow: They don't labor or spin thread. Yet I tell you, not even Solomon in all his splendor was adorned like one of these! If that's how God clothes the grass, which is in the field today and is thrown into the furnace tomorrow, how much more will He do for you—you of little faith?"
~ Luke 12:24–28

Give God the Glory

The people came up from the Jordan on the tenth day of the first month, and camped at Gilgal on the eastern limits of Jericho. Then Joshua set up in Gilgal the 12 stones they had taken from the Jordan, and he said to the Israelites, "In the future, when your children ask their fathers, 'What is the meaning of these stones?' you should tell your children,

'Israel crossed the Jordan on dry ground.' For the LORD your God dried up the waters of the Jordan before you until you had crossed over, just as the LORD your God did to the Red Sea, which He dried up before us until we had crossed over. This is so that all the people of the earth may know that the LORD's hand is mighty, and so that you may always fear the LORD your God." ~ Joshua 4:19–24

Shaped by God

This is the word that came to Jeremiah from the LORD: "Go down at once to the potter's house; there I will reveal My words to you." So I went down to the potter's house, and there he was, working away at the wheel. But the jar that he was making from the clay became flawed in the potter's hand, so he made it into another jar, as it seemed right for him to do.

The word of the LORD came to me: "House of Israel, can I not treat you as this potter treats his clay?"—this is the LORD's declaration. "Just like clay in the potter's hand, so are you in My hand, house of Israel." ~ Jeremiah 18:1–6

Prayer

Lord, be with me as I prepare to teach today. Strengthen me in wisdom and help me to shine Your light on my students. Amen.

Chapter 2

LET GOD BE
YOUR GUIDE

Charles Spurgeon reminded us that when we seek God's guidance, it's helpful to do it this way. "What would Jesus do?" and then think of another—"How would Jesus do it?" for what Jesus would do, and how He would do it, may always stand as the best guide to us.

As a teacher, it's not always easy to know the best course of action, either in the way that you help students master a concept, or the way you handle a situation that is somewhat out of the ordinary. Yet, you're called upon to do those very things daily and it's a blessing to realize that God is truly with you in every situation. God is your able and ready guide.

You've been called to teach and serve as an ambassador of grace and as one who works to meet a variety of needs in every student, and you know the monumental task at hand. Your job is to do more than educate. Your job is to equip your students for life. As John Donne so aptly put it, "Our critical day is not the very day of our death, but the whole course of life; I thank them, that pray for me when my bell tolls; but I thank them much more, that catechize me, or preach to me, or instruct me how to live."

As you instruct your students today, know that God is beside you, guiding you in all you do.

The Bible Promises . . .

Teach Your Children

> These words that I am giving you today are to be in your heart. Repeat them to your children. Talk about them when you sit in your house and when you walk along the road, when you lie down and when you get up. Bind them as a sign on your hand and let them be a symbol on

your forehead. Write them on the doorposts of your house and on your gates.
~ Deuteronomy 6:6–9

Generation to Generation

Tell your children about it, and let your children tell their children, and their children the next generation. ~ Joel 1:3

The Lamp

Your word is a lamp for my feet and a light on my path. ~ Psalm 119:105

The Honor of Teaching

The elders who are good leaders should be considered worthy of an ample honorarium, especially those who work hard at preaching and teaching. ~ 1 Timothy 5:17

God's Direction

> Trust in the Lord with all your heart,
> and do not rely on your own understand-
> ing; think about Him in all your ways,
> and He will guide you on the right paths.
> ~ Proverbs 3:5–6

God Supplies Your Needs

> And my God will supply all your needs
> according to His riches in glory in Christ
> Jesus. ~ Philippians 4:19

God is always near you and with you;
leave Him not alone. ~ Brother Lawrence

God Gives You Wisdom

> But it is from Him that you are in Christ
> Jesus, who became God-given wisdom
> for us—our righteousness, sanctification,
> and redemption. ~ 1 Corinthians 1:30

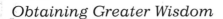

Obtaining Greater Wisdom

There will be times of security for you—a storehouse of salvation, wisdom, and knowledge. The fear of the LORD is Zion's treasure. ~ Isaiah 33:6

Providence has at all times been my only dependence, for all other resources seem to have failed us.
~ George Washington

Building a Foundation

My aim is to evangelize where Christ has not been named, so that I will not build on someone else's foundation. ~ Romans 15:20

All the scholastic scaffolding falls, as a ruined edifice, before one single word . . . faith. ~ Napoleon Bonaparte

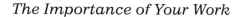

The Importance of Your Work

For no one can lay any other foundation than what has been laid down. That foundation is Jesus Christ. If anyone builds on that foundation with gold, silver, costly stones, wood, hay, or straw, each one's work will become obvious, for the day will disclose it, because it will be revealed by fire; the fire will test the quality of each one's work. If anyone's work that he has built survives, he will receive a reward. ~ 1 Corinthians 3:11–14

Becoming God's Vessel

Now in a large house there are not only gold and silver bowls, but also those of wood and clay, some for honorable use, some for dishonorable. So if anyone purifies himself from anything dishonorable, he will be a special instrument, set apart, useful to the Master, prepared for every good work. ~ 2 Timothy 2:20–21

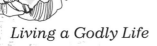

Living a Godly Life

For the grace of God has appeared with salvation for all people, instructing us to deny godlessness and worldly lusts and to live in a sensible, righteous, and godly way in the present age. ~ Titus 2:11–12

Sowing Goodness

Don't be deceived: God is not mocked. For whatever a man sows he will also reap, because the one who sows to his flesh will reap corruption from the flesh, but the one who sows to the Spirit will reap eternal life from the Spirit. ~ Galatians 6:7–8

God Lifts You Up

Humble yourselves, therefore, under the mighty hand of God, so that He may exalt you at the proper time, casting all your care on Him, because He cares about you. ~ 1 Peter 5:6-7

Embracing God

I will sow her in the land for Myself, and I will have compassion on No Compassion; I will say to Not My People: You are My people, and he will say, "You are My God." ~ Hosea 2:23

The Samaritan in You

Just then an expert in the law stood up to test Him, saying, "Teacher, what must I do to inherit eternal life?"

"What is written in the law?" He asked him. "How do you read it?"

He answered:

Love the Lord your God with all your heart, with all your soul, with all your strength, and with all your mind; and your neighbor as yourself.
~ Luke 10:25–27

Keep Praying

Don't worry about anything, but in everything, through prayer and petition with thanksgiving, let your requests be made known to God. ~ Philippians 4:6

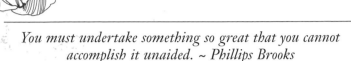

You must undertake something so great that you cannot accomplish it unaided. ~ Phillips Brooks

You Have the Victory

Because whatever has been born of God conquers the world. This is the victory that has conquered the world: our faith. And who is the one who conquers the world but the one who believes that Jesus is the Son of God? ~ 1 John 5:4–5

Guided by Faith

Now faith is the reality of what is hoped for, the proof of what is not seen.
~ Hebrews 11:1

God does not keep an extra supply of goodness that is higher than faith, and there is no help at all in anything that is below it. Within faith is where the Lord wants us to stay. ~ Julian of Norwich

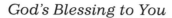

God's Blessing to You

How happy are those whose way is blameless, who live according to the Lord's instruction! Happy are those who keep His decrees and seek Him with all their heart. They do nothing wrong; they follow His ways. You have commanded that Your precepts be diligently kept. If only my ways were committed to keeping Your statutes! ~ Psalm 119:1–5

Knowing Whom You Serve

"No one can be a slave of two masters, since either he will hate one and love the other, or be devoted to one and despise the other. You cannot be slaves of God and of money." ~ Matthew 6:24

You may easily be too big for God to use, but never too small. ~ Dwight L. Moody

---

Follow My Example

> Imitate me, as I also imitate Christ.
> ~ 1 Corinthians 11:1

Knowing Whom You Believe

> And that is why I suffer these things. But
> I am not ashamed, because I know the
> One I have believed in and am persuaded
> that He is able to guard what has been
> entrusted to me until that day.
> ~ 2 Timothy 1:12

Prayer

Lord, thank You for being with me every day. Guide me as I teach, stay close to me and provide the wisdom to help my students grow in ways that please You. Help me to always encourage their hearts and stimulate their minds. Amen.

Chapter 3

LEAD BY TRUTH
AND EXAMPLE

If you think back on your own experience of education, whether you're thinking of formal education or life lessons, you probably realize that the best teachers were those who taught you through example. The people who demonstrated the principles that gave meaning to their words, most likely had the greatest impact on you. You not only remember what they said, but you remember the joy you felt in understanding something for the first time, of actually grasping a concept that had once been foreign.

Jesus taught by example and by story. He demonstrated the ways to live and the way to treat others. He loved people right where He found them. Teachers do the same thing. They lead by example and they share the truth of their hearts and the knowledge of their experience of life. You have an incredible impact on others and you're important to those whom you serve so well.

God blesses your work and seeks to strengthen and renew you in it each and every day.

The Bible Promises . . .

Follow His Steps

> For you were called to this, because
> Christ also suffered for you, leaving you
> an example, so that you should follow in
> His steps. ~ 1 Peter 2:21

---

*The first gift we can bestow on others is
a good example. ~ Thomas Morell*

Learn God's Ways Yourself

> And if you are convinced that you are
> a guide for the blind, a light to those in

darkness, an instructor of the ignorant, a teacher of the immature, having the full expression of knowledge and truth in the law— you then, who teach another, don't you teach yourself? You who preach, "You must not steal"—do you steal? You who say, "You must not commit adultery"—do you commit adultery? You who detest idols, do you rob their temples? You who boast in the law, do you dishonor God by breaking the law?
~ Romans 2:19–23

The gulf between knowledge and truth is infinite.
~ Henry Miller

Teach Sound Doctrine

So if you have been raised with the Messiah, seek what is above, where the Messiah is, seated at the right hand of God. Set your minds on what is above, not on what is on the earth. For you have died, and your life is hidden with the Messiah in God. When the Messiah, who is your life, is revealed, then you also will be revealed with Him in glory.

Therefore, put to death what belongs to your worldly nature: sexual immorality, impurity, lust, evil desire, and greed, which is idolatry. Because of these, God's wrath comes on the disobedient, and you once walked in these things when you were living in them. But now you must also put away all the following: anger, wrath, malice, slander, and filthy language from your mouth. Do not lie to one another, since you have put off the old self with its practices

Therefore, God's chosen ones, holy and loved, put on heartfelt compassion, kindness, humility, gentleness, and patience, accepting one another and forgiving one another if anyone has a complaint against another. Just as the Lord has forgiven you, so you must also forgive. Above all, put on love—the perfect bond of unity. And let the peace of the Messiah, to which you were also called in one body, control your hearts. Be thankful. Let the message about the Messiah dwell richly among you, teaching and admonishing one another in all

wisdom, and singing psalms, hymns, and spiritual songs, with gratitude in your hearts to God. And whatever you do, in word or in deed, do everything in the name of the Lord Jesus, giving thanks to God the Father through Him.
~ Colossians 3:1–9, 12–17

Truth is the foundation of all knowledge and the cement of all societies. ~ John Dryden

---

Be Wise

But you must say the things that are consistent with sound teaching. Older men are to be level headed, worthy of respect, sensible, and sound in faith, love, and endurance. In the same way, older women are to be reverent in behavior, not slanderers, not addicted to much wine. They are to teach what is good, so they may encourage the young women to love their husbands and to love their children, to be self-controlled, pure, homemakers, kind, and submissive to their husbands, so that God's message will not be slandered.

In the same way, encourage the young men to be self-controlled in everything. Make yourself an example of good works with integrity and dignity in your teaching. Your message is to be sound beyond reproach, so that the opponent will be ashamed, having nothing bad to say about us.

Slaves are to be submissive to their masters in everything, and to be well-pleasing, not talking back or stealing, but demonstrating utter faithfulness, so that they may adorn the teaching of God our Savior in everything. ~ Titus 2:1–10

If a million people believe a foolish thing, it is still a foolish thing. ~ Anatole France

---

Hold Fast to Truth

Hold on to the pattern of sound teaching that you have heard from me, in the faith and love that are in Christ Jesus. Guard,

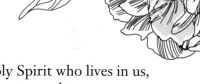

through the Holy Spirit who lives in us,
that good thing entrusted to you.
~ 2 Timothy 1:13–14

Truth is the first chapter in the book of wisdom.
~ Thomas Jefferson

Setting an example is not the main means
of influencing others, it is the only means.
~ Albert Einstein

Love the Truth

"The LORD of Hosts says this: The fast
of the fourth month, the fast of the fifth,
the fast of the seventh, and the fast of the
tenth will become times of joy, gladness,
and cheerful festivals for the house of
Judah. Therefore, love truth and peace."
~ Zechariah 8:19

Witness to Truth

"You are a king then?" Pilate asked.
"You say that I'm a king," Jesus
replied. "I was born for this, and I have
come into the world for this: to testify to
the truth. Everyone who is of the truth
listens to My voice." ~ John 18:37

---

*Example is the school of mankind, and they will learn
at no other. ~ Edmund Burke*

The Joy of Walking in Truth

I have no greater joy than this: to hear
that my children are walking in the truth.
~ 3 John 4

---

*The quality of a person's life is in direct proportion
to their commitment to excellence, regardless of their
chosen field of endeavor. ~ Vince Lombardi*

Think on These Things

> Finally brothers, whatever is true, whatever is honorable, whatever is just, whatever is pure, whatever is lovely, whatever is commendable—if there is any moral excellence and if there is any praise—dwell on these things. ~ Philippians 4:8

Let us preach you, Dear Jesus, without preaching . . . not by words but by our example . . . by the casting force, the sympathetic influence of what we do, the evident fullness of the love our hearts bear to you. Amen. ~ Mother Teresa

Prayer

Dear Lord, Help me to always be a worthy example of Your love, Your infinite wisdom, and Your grace. Let me never compromise Your truths and confuse my students with philosophies that cannot offer them renewed strength to seek the best from You and from life. Guide me, Lord, into the ways of Your truth. Amen.

Chapter 4

GET TO KNOW ALL YOUR STUDENTS

Paul Tournier once said, "You can never establish a personal relationship without opening up your own heart."

As a teacher, you aren't interested in establishing personal friendships with your students, but you are personally interested in their lives, because the more you know them, the better you understand how to teach them.

Schools are full of students who feel invisible, left to their own devices for good or ill because no one takes the time to really know who they are. Sure, taking the time is part of the issue, but teachers are not only sharing the knowledge of a particular field of study or a discipline, teachers are sharing the experience of life, pointing the way to something better. A teacher who seeks to identify the needs of the whole student is successful in educating the whole student.

Goethe said that "if you want people to be glad to meet you, you must be glad to meet them—and show it." Teachers have to be glad to meet their students and do all they can to meet them more than half way, because each student matters. Getting to know your students will serve you well. Getting to know your students will make you a better servant.

God bless you in your work today.

The Bible Promises . . .

Don't Look Down on Anyone

> "See that you don't look down on one of these little ones, because I tell you that in heaven their angels continually view the face of My Father in heaven." ~ Matthew 18:10

Give What You Have

> "And whoever gives just a cup of cold
> water to one of these little ones because
> he is a disciple—I assure you: He will
> never lose his reward!" ~ Matthew 10:42

---

*The person has achieved success who has loved much,
laughed often and been an inspiration to children.
~ Author Unknown*

Become Like a Child

At that time the disciples came to Jesus
and said, "Who is greatest in the kingdom of heaven?"

Then He called a child to Him and
had him stand among them. "I assure
you," He said, "unless you are converted
and become like children, you will never
enter the kingdom of heaven. Therefore, whoever humbles himself like this
child—this one is the greatest in the
kingdom of heaven. And whoever welcomes one child like this in My name
welcomes Me.

"But whoever causes the downfall of one of these little ones who believe in Me—it would be better for him if a heavy millstone were hung around his neck and he were drowned in the depths of the sea!" ~ Matthew 18:1–6

Let the Children Come to Me

Then children were brought to Him so He might put His hands on them and pray. But the disciples rebuked them. Then Jesus said, "Leave the children alone, and don't try to keep them from coming to Me, because the kingdom of heaven is made up of people like this." After putting His hands on them, He went on from there. ~ Matthew 19:13–15

Protect the Children

Now I am ready to come to you this third time. I will not burden you, for I am not seeking what is yours, but you. For children are not obligated to save up for their parents, but parents for their children. ~ 2 Corinthians 12:14

Generation to Generation

The counsel of the LORD stands forever,
the plans of His heart from generation to
generation. ~ Psalm 33:11

We are each of us angels with only one wing.
And we can only fly embracing each other.
~ Luciano De Creschenzo

Be Gentle

Although we could have been a burden as
Christ's apostles, instead we were gentle
among you, as a nursing mother nurtures
her own children. ~ 1 Thessalonians 2:7

Teaching in the Classroom

Moses commanded them, "At the end
of every seven years, at the appointed
time in the year of debt cancellation,
during the Festival of Booths, when all
Israel assembles in the presence of the
LORD your God at the place He chooses,

you are to read this law aloud before all Israel. Gather the people—men, women, children, and foreigners living within your gates—so that they may listen and learn to fear the LORD your God and be careful to follow all the words of this law. Then their children who do not know the law will listen and learn to fear the LORD your God as long as you live in the land you are crossing the Jordan to possess." ~ Deuteronomy 31:10–13

We cannot live only for ourselves. A thousand fibers connect us with our fellow men! ~ *Herman Melville*

The Schoolmaster

The law, then, was our guardian until Christ, so that we could be justified by faith. But since that faith has come, we are no longer under a guardian.
~ Galatians 3:24–25

Four Steps to Achievement:
Plan purposefully
Prepare prayerfully
Proceed positively
Pursue Persistently
~ William A. Ward

Setting Hope in God

My people, hear my instruction; listen to what I say. I will declare wise sayings; I will speak mysteries from the past—things we have heard and known and that our fathers have passed down to us. We must not hide them from their children, but must tell a future generation the praises of the Lord, His might, and the wonderful works He has performed. He established a testimony in Jacob and set up a law in Israel, which He commanded our fathers to teach to their children so that a future generation—children yet to be born —might know. They were to rise and tell their children so that they might put their confidence in God and not forget God's works, but keep His commands. Then they would not be like their fathers, a stubborn and rebellious generation, a generation whose heart was not loyal and whose spirit was not faithful to God. ~ Psalm 78:1–8

The Lord Bless You

"Tell Aaron and his sons how you are to bless the Israelites. Say to them:

May Yahweh bless you and protect you; may Yahweh make His face shine on you and be gracious to you; may Yahweh look with favor on you and give you peace. ~ Numbers 6:23–26

The Lord Deal Kindly with You

She said to them, "Each of you go back to your mother's home. May the LORD show faithful love to you as you have shown to the dead and to me. May the LORD enable each of you to find security in the house of your new husband." She kissed them, and they wept loudly. ~ Ruth 1:8–9

Go and Teach Others

Then Jesus came near and said to them,
"All authority has been given to Me in
heaven and on earth. Go, therefore, and
make disciples of all nations, baptizing
them in the name of the Father and of
the Son and of the Holy Spirit, teaching
them to observe everything I have commanded you. And remember, I am with
you always, to the end of the age."
~ Matthew 28:18–20

Unless we do his teachings, we do not demonstrate
faith in him. ~ Ezra Taft Benson

God's Anointing

The Spirit of the Lord is on Me, because
He has anointed Me to preach good
news to the poor. He has sent Me to
proclaim freedom to the captives
and recovery of sight to the blind, to set
free the oppressed, to proclaim the year
of the Lord's favor.

He then rolled up the scroll, gave it back to the attendant, and sat down. And the eyes of everyone in the synagogue were fixed on Him. He began by saying to them, "Today as you listen, this Scripture has been fulfilled." ~ Luke 4:18–21

God Is the Master

The rich and the poor have this in common: the LORD made them both. ~ Proverbs 22:2

Show No Partiality

There is no Jew or Greek, slave or free, male or female; for you are all one in Christ Jesus. And if you belong to Christ, then you are Abraham's seed, heirs according to the promise. ~ Galatians 3:28–29

God Treats Everyone the Same Way

Affliction and distress for every human being who does evil, first to the Jew, and also to the Greek; but glory, honor,

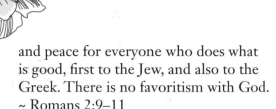

and peace for everyone who does what is good, first to the Jew, and also to the Greek. There is no favoritism with God. ~ Romans 2:9–11

Speak Kindly

A gentle answer turns away anger, but a harsh word stirs up wrath. ~ Proverbs 15:1

Children need models more than they need critics.
~ J. Joubert

Cheerful Givers

Remember this: The person who sows sparingly will also reap sparingly, and the person who sows generously will also reap generously. Each person should do as he has decided in his heart—not reluctantly or out of necessity, for God loves a cheerful giver. ~ 2 Corinthians 9:6–7

Be Quick to Listen

> My dearly loved brothers, understand
> this: Everyone must be quick to hear, slow
> to speak, and slow to anger. ~ James 1:19

The Golden Rule

> Therefore, whatever you want others to
> do for you, do also the same for them—
> this is the Law and the Prophets.
> ~ Matthew 7:12

---

*Small kindnesses, small courtesies, small considerations,
give a greater charm to the character than the display of
great talents and accomplishments. ~ Mary Ann Kelty*

Prayer

*Lord, You know each of the students who come
into my life and You know them well. Help me to get
to know them too so that I can influence, educate, and
guide them. I ask this in Jesus name, Amen.*

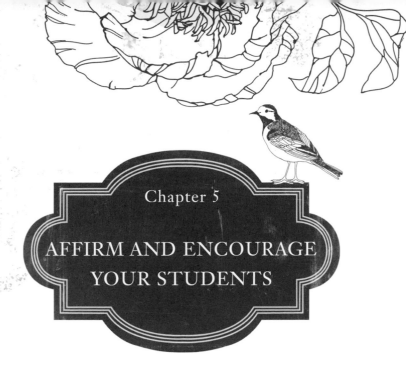

Chapter 5

AFFIRM AND ENCOURAGE YOUR STUDENTS

One of the greatest gifts any teacher can give students is as an encourager of their hopes and dreams. Your students need to know that you support their efforts, that you encourage their growth and potential and that you are willing to guide them if they start going in the wrong direction. You are the one who can influence them in positive ways and your smile, your affirmation, is what they need more than anything.

If you hope to be a successful teacher, than you want to be motivated by love, by a willingness to help your students set new goals and to push past even what they might expect from themselves. You're the catalyst of the future, the one who sees where they are and where they hope to go. Offer them your wisdom and your expertise, but also offer them your kindness and your counsel. God has placed you in their lives to make a difference and He trusts you to do your best each day.

You're an effective, strong, and inspiring teacher because somewhere along the way someone believed in you, affirmed you, and encouraged you to become the person you are today. That's the task at hand, the gift you have to offer.

God be with you in all you do in the classroom.

The Bible Promises . . .

A Favorable Response

> A man takes joy in giving an answer; and
> a timely word—how good that is!
> ~ Proverbs 15:23

True education doesn't merely bring us learning,
but love of learning; not merely work, but love of work.
~ Author Unknown

Hold Fast to What Is Good

But test all things. Hold on to what is good. ~ 1 Thessalonians 5:21

Train Up a Child

Teach a youth about the way he should go; even when he is old he will not depart from it. ~ Proverbs 22:6

The task of the modern educator is not to cut down jungles, but to irrigate deserts. ~ C. S. Lewis

---

Assurance

Let us draw near with a true heart in full assurance of faith, our hearts sprinkled clean from an evil conscience and our bodies washed in pure water. ~ Hebrews 10:22

Education is not the filling of a pail,
but the lighting of a fire. ~ William Butler Yeats

Pleasing God

Do not be conformed to this age, but
be transformed by the renewing of your
mind, so that you may discern what is the
good, pleasing, and perfect will of God.
~ Romans 12:2

Sing to the Lord

May the Lord add to your numbers,
both yours and your children's. May you
be blessed by the Lord, the Maker of
heaven and earth. The heavens are the
Lord's, but the earth He has given to the
human race. It is not the dead who praise
the Lord, nor any of those descending
into the silence of death. But we will
praise the Lord, both now and forever.
Hallelujah! ~ Psalm 115:14–18

Great Is the Lord

I exalt You, my God the King, and praise Your name forever and ever.

I will praise You every day; I will honor Your name forever and ever.

Yahweh is great and is highly praised; His greatness is unsearchable. One generation will declare Your works to the next and will proclaim Your mighty acts.
~ Psalm 145:1–4

Do Good

Therefore, whatever you want others to do for you, do also the same for them— this is the Law and the Prophets.
~ Matthew 7:12

Put on Light

The night is nearly over, and the daylight is near, so let us discard the deeds of darkness and put on the armor of light.
~ Romans 13:12

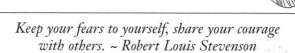

*Keep your fears to yourself, share your courage
with others. ~ Robert Louis Stevenson*

Do What Is Right

The one who pursues righteousness and
faithful love will find life, righteousness,
and honor. ~ Proverbs 21:21

*Too often we give our children answers to remember
rather than problems to solve. ~ Roger Lewin*

Saved by Grace

For you are saved by grace through
faith, and this is not from yourselves; it
is God's gift—not from works, so that no
one can boast. For we are His creation,
created in Christ Jesus for good works,
which God prepared ahead of time so
that we should walk in them. ~ Ephesians
2:8–10

Share with Others

> Don't neglect to do what is good and to share, for God is pleased with such sacrifices. ~ Hebrews 13:16

Treat people as if they were what they ought to be and you help them to become what they are capable of being. ~ Goethe

---

Be Cheerful Givers

> Remember this: The person who sows sparingly will also reap sparingly, and the person who sows generously will also reap generously. Each person should do as he has decided in his heart—not reluctantly or out of necessity, for God loves a cheerful giver. ~ 2 Corinthians 9:6–7

Friends Love at All Times

> A friend loves at all times, and a brother is born for a difficult time. ~ Proverbs 17:17

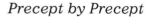

Precept by Precept

For he says: "Law after law, law after law, line after line, line after line, a little here, a little there." ~ Isaiah 28:10

Entertain Strangers

Don't neglect to show hospitality, for by doing this some have welcomed angels as guests without knowing it. ~ Hebrews 13:2

The really great teacher is the teacher who makes every student feel great. ~ Adapted from G. K. Chesterton

---

Offer Hospitality

Be hospitable to one another without complaining. ~ 1 Peter 4:9

---

*Encouragement is oxygen of the soul.
~ Author Unknown*

Conversations of Grace

> Your speech should always be gracious,
> seasoned with salt, so that you may know
> how you should answer each person.
> ~ Colossians 4:6

I praise loudly. I blame softly. ~ Catherine II of Russia

Bear with Each Other

> Accepting one another and forgiving one
> another if anyone has a complaint against
> another. Just as the Lord has forgiven
> you, so you must also forgive.
> ~ Colossians 3:13

God Knows the Details

> But even the hairs of your head have all
> been counted. ~ Matthew 10:30

> *To endure is the first thing that a child ought to learn, and that which he will have the most need to know. ~ Jean Jacques Rousseau*

Prayer

Lord, I thank You for the students You have brought my way. Help me to guide them with compassion, teach them with skill, and shine a light in their direction to brighten their steps. Amen.

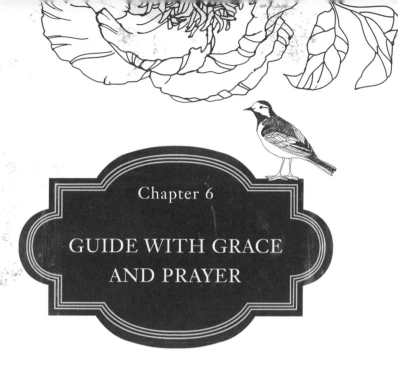

Chapter 6

GUIDE WITH GRACE AND PRAYER

There's an adage from conventional wisdom that reminds us that God sees where we are and loves us, but He loves us too much to leave us there. As a teacher, your job is to meet your students where they are, but with grace and prayer, be willing to guide them on to greater possibilities. You're there to keep them moving and growing into all God designed them to become.

That's not always an easy task and it takes the grace of God in your own life to help you do your job well. You have to remember that somewhere along the way, someone had enough patience to see you through, to guide you to your own next steps.

You and your students are going to have good days and bad days. As Jerry Bridges reminds us though, "Your worst days are never so bad that you are beyond the reach of God's grace. And your best days are never so good that you are beyond the need of God's grace."

Meet your students where they are and with grace and prayer, move them to the place that will make your heavenly Father proud.

God bless your work today!

The Bible Promises . . .

A Little Grace

> Now grace was given to each one of us according to the measure of the Messiah's gift. ~ Ephesians 4:7

Cheap grace is grace without discipleship, grace without the cross, grace without Jesus Christ, living and incarnate. Costly grace is the treasure hidden in the field; for the sake of it a man will gladly go and sell all that he has. ~ Dietrich Bonhoeffer

---

Speaking of Grace

Your speech should always be gracious,
seasoned with salt, so that you may know
how you should answer each person.
~ Colossians 4:6

Grace for you

The Lord be with your spirit. Grace be
with you. ~ 2 Timothy 4:22

---

*Grace is the gift of Christ, who exposes the gulf which
separates God and man, and, by exposing it, bridges it.
~ Karl Barth*

Preparing for Grace

LORD, my heart is not proud; my eyes
are not haughty. I do not get involved
with things too great or too difficult for
me. Instead, I have calmed and quieted
myself like a little weaned child with its
mother; I am like a little child.

Israel, put your hope in the LORD,
both now and forever. ~ Psalm 131:1–3

---

*A state of mind that sees God in everything is
evidence of growth in grace and a thankful heart.*
~ Charles Finney

Growing Up

"LORD my God, You have now made
Your servant king in my father David's
place. Yet I am just a youth with no experience in leadership." ~ 1 Kings 3:7

Gaining Wisdom

Brothers, don't be childish in your thinking, but be infants in regard to evil and
adult in your thinking. ~ 1 Corinthians
14:20

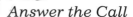

Answer the Call

But I protested, "Oh no, Lord, God! Look, I don't know how to speak since I am only a youth."

Then the Lord said to me:

Do not say, "I am only a youth," for you will go to everyone I send you to and speak whatever I tell you. Do not be afraid of anyone, for I will be with you to deliver you. This is the Lord's declaration. ~ Jeremiah 1:6–8

Serve the Lord

Shout triumphantly to the Lord, all the earth. Serve the Lord with gladness; come before Him with joyful songs. Acknowledge that Yahweh is God. He made us, and we are His—His people, the sheep of His pasture. Enter His gates with thanksgiving and His courts with praise. Give thanks to Him and praise His name. For Yahweh is good, and His love is eternal; His faithfulness endures through all generations. ~ Psalm 100:1–5

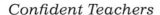

Confident Teachers

Proclaiming the kingdom of God and
teaching the things concerning the Lord
Jesus Christ with full boldness and without hindrance. ~ Acts 28:31

---

*If you are swept off your feet, it's time to get
on your knees. ~ Fred Beck*

Grace Abounds

And God is able to make every grace
overflow to you, so that in every way,
always having everything you need,
you may excel in every good work.
~ 2 Corinthians 9:8

---

*Grace is the free, undeserved goodness and favor
of God to mankind. ~ Matthew Henry*

This Present World

One of their very own prophets said,
Cretans are always liars, evil beasts, lazy
gluttons. ~ Titus 1:12

---

*Not only does understanding the gospel of the grace of
God provide a proper motive for us to share our faith,
it also gives us the proper motive and means to live the
Christian life effectively. ~ David Havard*

Singing with Grace

Let the message about the Messiah
dwell richly among you, teaching and
admonishing one another in all wisdom,
and singing psalms, hymns, and spiritual
songs, with gratitude in your hearts to
God. ~ Colossians 3:16

---

*There is nothing but God's grace. We walk upon it; we
breathe it; we live and die by it; it makes the nails and
axles of the universe. ~ Robert Louis Stevenson*

Gaining Knowledge

> But now, Job, pay attention to my speech,
> and listen to all my words. I am going to
> open my mouth; my tongue will form
> words on my palate. My words come
> from my upright heart, and my lips speak
> with sincerity what they know.
> ~ Job 33:1–3

*Our prayers are answered not when we are
given what we ask but when we are challenged
to be what we can be. ~ Morris Alder*

A Good Word

> A man takes joy in giving an answer; and
> a timely word—how good that is!
> ~ Proverbs 15:23

*Prayer is not conquering God's reluctance, but taking
hold of God's willingness. ~ Phillips Brooks*

Preparing for the Future

Who may ascend the mountain of the LORD? Who may stand in His holy place? The one who has clean hands and a pure heart, who has not set his mind on what is false, and who has not sworn deceitfully. ~ Psalm 24:3–4

Speaking Truth

But speaking the truth in love, let us grow in every way into Him who is the head—Christ. From Him the whole body, fitted and knit together by every supporting ligament, promotes the growth of the body for building up itself in love by the proper working of each individual part. ~ Ephesians 4:15–16

Prayer is a sincere, sensible, affectionate pouring out of the soul to God, through Christ in the strength and assistance of the Spirit, for such things as God has promised. ~ John Bunyan

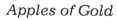

Apples of Gold

A word spoken at the right time is like gold apples on a silver tray. A wise correction to a receptive ear is like a gold ring or an ornament of gold.

To those who send him, a trustworthy messenger is like the coolness of snow on a harvest day; he refreshes the life of his masters.

The man who boasts about a gift that does not exist is like clouds and wind without rain. A ruler can be persuaded through patience, and a gentle tongue can break a bone. ~ Proverbs 25:11–15

Pray for Those You Teach

And I pray this: that your love will keep on growing in knowledge and every kind of discernment. ~ Philippians 1:9

Pray as if everything depended on your prayer.
~ William Booth

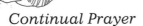

Continual Prayer

For this reason also, since the day we heard this, we haven't stopped praying for you. We are asking that you may be filled with the knowledge of His will in all wisdom and spiritual understanding, so that you may walk worthy of the Lord, fully pleasing to Him, bearing fruit in every good work and growing in the knowledge of God. May you be strengthened with all power, according to His glorious might, for all endurance and patience, with joy. ~ Colossians 1:9–11

None can believe how powerful prayer is, and what it is able to effect, but those who have learned it by experience. ~ Martin Luther

---

Finding the Righteous

Then the LORD said, "The outcry against Sodom and Gomorrah is immense, and their sin is extremely serious. I will go down to see if what they have done justifies the cry that has come up to Me. If not, I will find out."

The men turned from there and went toward Sodom while Abraham remained standing before the LORD. Abraham stepped forward and said, "Will You really sweep away the righteous with the wicked? What if there are 50 righteous people in the city? Will You really sweep it away instead of sparing the place for the sake of the 50 righteous people who are in it? You could not possibly do such a thing: to kill the righteous with the wicked, treating the righteous and the wicked alike. You could not possibly do that! Won't the Judge of all the earth do what is just?" ~ Genesis 18:20–25

The pure prayer that ascends from a faithful heart will be like incense rising from a hallowed altar.
~ Augustine of Hippo

68

Prayer

Lord, You know that I cannot teach without Your grace and mercy, and I cannot guide my students well without Your help. Be with me and with those I seek to guide in all that I do today. Amen.

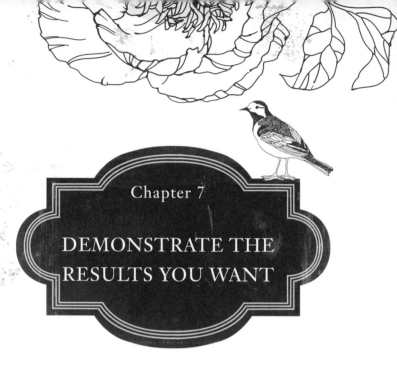

Chapter 7

DEMONSTRATE THE RESULTS YOU WANT

As a teacher, you're used to using object lessons and giving demonstrations to clarify a concept. You want your students to not only get an understanding of the final result, but to actually experience the process so that the end result will stay with them for a long time.

Whether you realize it or not, you're Exhibit A, the one actual evidence your students have for where they hope to go in life. They have your example and your expertise to serve as a model and an inspiration. When you share your thoughts and ideas, your students are getting a lot more information than just a few simple facts to digest and recall on the next exam.

Goethe said, "If you would create something, you must be something." As a teacher you are something. You're a shining example of God's love and desire to create a greater blessing for all humankind. You're a demonstration of His love.

Praise God today for the great work He has begun in you.

The Bible Promises . . .

God's Demonstration of Power

> After this I will pour out My Spirit on all humanity; then your sons and your daughters will prophesy, your old men will have dreams, and your young men will see visions. I will even pour out My Spirit on the male and female slaves in those days. I will display wonders in the heavens and on the earth: blood, fire, and columns of smoke. The sun will be turned to darkness and the moon to blood before the great and awe inspiring Day of the LORD comes. Then everyone

who calls on the name of Yahweh will be saved, for there will be an escape for those on Mount Zion and in Jerusalem, as the LORD promised, among the survivors the LORD calls. ~ Joel 2:28–32

The Gift of the Holy Spirit

"If you then, who are evil, know how to give good gifts to your children, how much more will the heavenly Father give the Holy Spirit to those who ask Him?" ~ Luke 11:13

Thirsty

On the last and most important day of the festival, Jesus stood up and cried out, "If anyone is thirsty, he should come to Me and drink! The one who believes in Me, as the Scripture has said, will have streams of living water flow from deep within him." He said this about the Spirit. Those who believed in Jesus were going to receive the Spirit, for the Spirit had not yet been received because Jesus had not yet been glorified. ~ John 7:37–39

How You Know the Spirit

And I will ask the Father, and He will give you another Counselor to be with you forever. He is the Spirit of truth. The world is unable to receive Him because it doesn't see Him or know Him. But you do know Him, because He remains with you and will be in you. ~ John 14:16–17

The Demonstration of Peace

But the Counselor, the Holy Spirit—the Father will send Him in My name—will teach you all things and remind you of everything I have told you. "Peace I leave with you. My peace I give to you. I do not give to you as the world gives. Your heart must not be troubled or fearful." ~ John 14:26–27

God Speaks through You

"Look, I'm sending you out like sheep among wolves. Therefore be as shrewd as serpents and as harmless as doves. Because people will hand you over to sanhedrins and flog you in their

synagogues, beware of them. You will even be brought before governors and kings because of Me, to bear witness to them and to the nations. But when they hand you over, don't worry about how or what you should speak. For you will be given what to say at that hour, because you are not speaking, but the Spirit of your Father is speaking through you."
~ Matthew 10:16–20

If we want a love message to be heard, it has to be sent out. To keep a lamp burning, we have to keep putting oil in it. ~ Mother Teresa

Remember What I Taught You

"I have told you these things to keep you from stumbling. They will ban you from the synagogues. In fact, a time is coming when anyone who kills you will think he is offering service to God. They will do these things because they haven't known the Father or Me. But I have told you these things so that when their time

comes you may remember I told them to you. I didn't tell you these things from the beginning, because I was with you."
~ John 16:1–4

The great end of life is not knowledge but action.
~ Thomas H. Huxley

Trials of Faith

You rejoice in this, though now for a short time you have had to struggle in various trials so that the genuineness of your faith—more valuable than gold, which perishes though refined by fire—may result in praise, glory, and honor at the revelation of Jesus Christ. ~ 1 Peter 1:6–7

Called by God

For God has not given us a spirit of fearfulness, but one of power, love, and sound judgment. So don't be ashamed of the testimony about our Lord, or of

me His prisoner. Instead, share in suffering for the gospel, relying on the power of God. He has saved us and called us with a holy calling, not according to our works, but according to His own purpose and grace, which was given to us in Christ Jesus before time began.
~ 2 Timothy 1:7–9

You can't build a reputation on what you're going to do. ~ Henry Ford

Striving for a Goal

Share in suffering as a good soldier of Christ Jesus. No one serving as a soldier gets entangled in the concerns of civilian life; he seeks to please the recruiter. Also, if anyone competes as an athlete, he is not crowned unless he competes according to the rules. ~ 2 Timothy 2:3–5

Lord, grant that I may always desire more than I accomplish. ~ Michelangelo

Salt and Light

"You are the salt of the earth. But if the salt should lose its taste, how can it be made salty? It's no longer good for anything but to be thrown out and trampled on by men." ~ Matthew 5:13

Act as if what you do makes a difference. It does.
~ William James

Let Your Light Shine

In the same way, let your light shine before men, so that they may see your good works and give glory to your Father in heaven. ~ Matthew 5:16

Unless we do his teachings, we do not demonstrate
faith in him. ~ Ezra Taft Benson

Teach Us

Teach us to number our days carefully so that we may develop wisdom in our hearts. ~ Psalm 90:12

Getting Understanding

Wisdom is supreme—so get wisdom. And whatever else you get, get understanding. ~ Proverbs 4:7

Take a method and try it. If it fails, admit it frankly, and try another. But by all means, try something.
~ F. D. Roosevelt

Wisdom and Knowledge

Get wisdom—how much better it is than gold! And get understanding—it is preferable to silver. ~ Proverbs 16:16

Knowing is not enough, we must apply. Willing is not enough, we must do. ~ Goethe

The Wisdom of the World

> For the wisdom of this world is foolishness with God, since it is written: He catches the wise in their craftiness; and again, The Lord knows that the reasonings of the wise are meaningless.
> ~ 1 Corinthians 3:19–20

Prayer

Dear Lord, Help me to always demonstrate Your kindness, Your mercy, and Your love to the students in my life. Help me seek the best possible outcome for each of them in any way that I can. Amen.

Chapter 8

TAKE CARE OF YOURSELF

It may seem somewhat glib to offer a comment to someone like "take care of yourself." Though it is a wise choice to make for yourself, you push on day after day giving all you can, challenging your stamina and your health even knowing at times that you might put those things in jeopardy.

The airlines remind you each time you take a flight that if the need arises, to always put on your oxygen mask before you try to help others. If you can't breathe, you can't be very effective to those around you. Teachers can forget to breathe, forget to take care of themselves. You're reminded today that as important as your students are, as great as your work is, it can only happen if you're properly rested, nourished, and fed. You must take care of yourself.

Consider the advice you would give one of your students, the wisdom you would offer about the difference a good night's sleep can make, or the right nutrition balance can bring. Consider this a "physician, heal thyself" day . . . a chance for you to breathe in all that God wants just for you.

The Bible Promises . . .

I Am the Vine

> "I am the vine; you are the branches. The one who remains in Me and I in him produces much fruit, because you can do nothing without Me." ~ John 15:5

Let your lives adorn your faith, let your example adorn your creed. Above all live in Christ Jesus and walk in Him, giving credence to no teaching but that which is manifestly approved of Him, and owned by the Holy Spirit. Cleave fast to the Word of God.
~ C. H. Spurgeon

Abba, Father!

And because you are sons, God has sent the Spirit of His Son into our hearts, crying, "Abba, Father!" ~ Galatians 4:6

The Golden Rule

Therefore, whatever you want others to do for you, do also the same for them— this is the Law and the Prophets. ~ Matthew 7:12

Counselors

Without guidance, people fall, but with many counselors there is deliverance. ~ Proverbs 11:14

God's Deliverance

Many adversities come to the one who is righteous, but the Lord delivers him from them all. ~ Psalm 34:19

Seek First His Kingdom

But seek first the kingdom of God and
His righteousness, and all these things
will be provided for you. ~ Matthew 6:33

---

*There is only one way to bring up a child in the way he
should go and that is to travel that way yourself.
~ Abraham Lincoln*

Lead a Quiet Life

To seek to lead a quiet life, to mind your
own business, and to work with your own
hands, as we commanded you.
~ 1 Thessalonians 4:11

---

*Reflect upon your present blessings—of which every
man has many—not on your past misfortunes, of which
all men have some. ~ Charles Dickens*

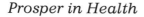

Prosper in Health

Dear friend, I pray that you may prosper in every way and be in good health physically just as you are spiritually.
~ 3 John 2

Day of Rest

You are to present to the LORD every firstborn male of the womb. All firstborn offspring of the livestock you own that are males will be the LORD's. ~ Exodus 13:12

Do what you can, with what you have, where you are.
~ Theodore Roosevelt

Obedience

Daniel determined that he would not defile himself with the king's food or with the wine he drank. So he asked permission from the chief official not to defile himself.

He agreed with them about this and tested them for 10 days. At the end of 10 days they looked better and healthier than all the young men who were eating the king's food. ~ Daniel 1:8, 14–15

We all want progress, but if you're on the wrong road, progress means doing an about—turn and walking back to the right road; in that case, the one who turns back the soonest is the most progressive. ~ C. S. Lewis

---

The Kingdom Is Not Food

For the kingdom of God is not eating and drinking, but righteousness, peace, and joy in the Holy Spirit. ~ Romans 14:17

Sleep

I lie down and sleep; I wake again because the LORD sustains me. ~ Psalm 3:5

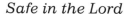

Safe in the Lord

Be angry and do not sin; on your bed,
reflect in your heart and be still. Selah
Offer sacrifices in righteousness and trust
in the Lord.

Many are saying, "Who can show us
anything good?" Look on us with favor,
Lord.

You have put more joy in my heart
than they have when their grain and new
wine abound. I will both lie down and
sleep in peace, for You alone, Lord, make
me live in safety. ~ Psalm 4:4–8

---

*Everything that a man leans upon but God, will be a
dart that will certainly pierce his heart through and
through. He who leans only upon Christ, lives the
highest, choicest, safest, and sweetest life.
~ Thomas Brooks*

God Cares about You

So God created man in His own image;
He created him in the image of God; He
created them male and female.

God blessed them, and God said to them, "Be fruitful, multiply, fill the earth, and subdue it. Rule the fish of the sea, the birds of the sky, and every creature that crawls on the earth." God also said, "Look, I have given you every seed—bearing plant on the surface of the entire earth and every tree whose fruit contains seed. This food will be for you."
~ Genesis 1:27–29

Wonderfully Made

I will praise You because I have been remarkably and wonderfully made. Your works are wonderful, and I know this very well. My bones were not hidden from You when I was made in secret, when I was formed in the depths of the earth. Your eyes saw me when I was formless; all my days were written in Your book and planned before a single one of them began. ~ Psalm 139:14–16

I am only one; but still I am one. I cannot do everything, but still I can do something; I will not refuse to do the something I can do. ~ Helen Keller

Fisher of Men

When daybreak came, Jesus stood on the shore. However, the disciples did not know it was Jesus.

"Men," Jesus called to them, "you don't have any fish, do you?"

"No," they answered.

"Cast the net on the right side of the boat," He told them, "and you'll find some." So they did, and they were unable to haul it in because of the large number of fish. Therefore the disciple, the one Jesus loved, said to Peter, "It is the Lord!"

When Simon Peter heard that it was the Lord, he tied his outer garment around him (for he was stripped) and plunged into the sea. But since they were not far from land (about 100 yards away), the other disciples came in the boat, dragging the net full of fish. When they got out on land, they saw a charcoal fire there, with fish lying on it, and bread.

"Bring some of the fish you've just caught," Jesus told them. So Simon Peter got up and hauled the net ashore, full of large fish—153 of them. Even though there were so many, the net was not torn.

"Come and have breakfast," Jesus told them. None of the disciples dared ask Him, "Who are You?" because they knew it was the Lord. Jesus came, took the bread, and gave it to them. He did the same with the fish. ~ John 21:4–13

Jesus accepts you the way you are, but loves you too much to leave you that way. ~ Lee Venden

---

God's Workmanship

For we are His creation, created in Christ Jesus for good works, which God prepared ahead of time so that we should walk in them. ~ Ephesians 2:10

Cast Your Cares on Him

> Casting all your care on Him, because
> He cares about you. ~ 1 Peter 5:7

The object of love is to serve, not to win.
~ Woodrow Wilson

Prayer

Lord, I thank You for Your divine hand in my life, Your willingness to shape and mold me and create in me the person you want Me to be. Help me to be willing to listen for Your voice so I can be a wise and inspiring teacher. Amen.

Chapter 9

LOVE EVERY MOMENT

No matter how much you may love what you do or how effective you may feel you are with your students, chances are you don't "love every moment." Love every moment is right up there with "pray without ceasing," something that seems almost impossible. How do we learn to love what is in front of us right now? How do we appreciate the process that takes us to the outcome we hope so much to achieve?

Start with this moment right now. Begin to see every moment as a gift from God, as an opportunity to grow and change. Let this be the moment when you say, "yes," to everything He plans for you. Every moment you give God your best is a moment you can love.

As a teacher, you get to love the moments, because in some of those "ah-ha's" extraordinary things are happening. In some of those moments, the light is coming on for your students in whole new ways. God is shining His light on you and people are being changed forever.

Love every moment that you let your light shine.

The Bible Promises . . .

Don't Grow Weary

> So we must not get tired of doing good, for we will reap at the proper time if we don't give up. ~ Galatians 6:9

In the rush and noise of life, as you have intervals, step home within yourselves and be still. Wait upon God, and feel his good presence; this will carry you evenly through your day's business. ~ William Penn

God's Strength

But He said to me, "My grace is sufficient for you, for power is perfected in weakness." Therefore, I will most gladly boast all the more about my weaknesses, so that Christ's power may reside in me. So I take pleasure in weaknesses, insults, catastrophes, persecutions, and in pressures, because of Christ. For when I am weak, then I am strong. ~ 2 Corinthians 12:9–10

Trust in the Lord

You will keep the mind that is dependent on You in perfect peace, for it is trusting in You. Trust in the LORD forever, because in Yah, the LORD, is an everlasting rock! ~ Isaiah 26:3–4

Bearing Fruit

He will be like a tree planted by water: it sends its roots out toward a stream, it doesn't fear when heat comes, and its foliage remains green. It will not worry

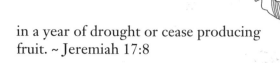

in a year of drought or cease producing fruit. ~ Jeremiah 17:8

Our greatest need is to teach people who think—not what, but how! ~ Thomas Edison

---

Stormy Moments

One day He and His disciples got into a boat, and He told them, "Let's cross over to the other side of the lake." So they set out, and as they were sailing He fell asleep. Then a fierce windstorm came down on the lake; they were being swamped and were in danger. They came and woke Him up, saying, "Master, Master, we're going to die!" Then He got up and rebuked the wind and the raging waves. So they ceased, and there was a calm. He said to them, "Where is your faith?"

They were fearful and amazed, asking one another, "Who can this be? He commands even the winds and the waves, and they obey Him!" ~ Luke 8:22–25

A prudent question is one half of wisdom.
~ Francis Bacon

Be Content

I don't say this out of need, for I have
learned to be content in whatever circumstances I am. I know both how to
have a little, and I know how to have a
lot. In any and all circumstances I have
learned the secret of being content—
whether well fed or hungry, whether in
abundance or in need. I am able to do
all things through Him who strengthens
me. ~ Philippians 4:11–13

There is within every soul a thirst for happiness and
meaning. ~ Thomas Aquinas

Go to the Rock

I am at rest in God alone; my salvation
comes from Him. He alone is my rock

and my salvation, my stronghold; I will
never be shaken. ~ Psalm 62:1–2

Wait Patiently for the Lord

I waited patiently for the LORD, and He
turned to me and heard my cry for help.
He brought me up from a desolate pit,
out of the muddy clay, and set my feet
on a rock, making my steps secure. He
put a new song in my mouth, a hymn of
praise to our God. Many will see and fear
and put their trust in the LORD. ~ Psalm
40:1–3

Pray without Ceasing

Rejoice always! Pray constantly. Give
thanks in everything, for this is God's
will for you in Christ Jesus.
~ 1 Thessalonians 5:16–18

Give Thanks

Give thanks to the LORD, for He is good;
His faithful love endures forever. ~ Psalm
118:1

Watch your thoughts; they become words.
Watch your words; they become actions.
Watch your actions; they become habits.
Watch your habits; they become character.
Watch your character; for it becomes your destiny.
~ Author Unknown

This Is the Day the Lord Has Made

This is the day the LORD has made; let us rejoice and be glad in it. ~ Psalm 118:24

God Gives Us Light

The LORD is God and has given us light. Bind the festival sacrifice with cords to the horns of the altar. ~ Psalm 118:27

For Everything There Is a Season

There is an occasion for everything, and a time for every activity under heaven: a time to give birth and a time to die; a time to plant and a time to uproot; a time to kill and a time to heal; a time to

tear down and a time to build; a time
to weep and a time to laugh; a time to
mourn and a time to dance; a time to
throw stones and a time to gather stones;
a time to embrace and a time to avoid
embracing; a time to search and a time to
count as lost; a time to keep and a time
to throw away; a time to tear and a time
to sew; a time to be silent and a time to
speak; a time to love and a time to hate; a
time for war and a time for peace.
~ Ecclesiastes 3:1–8

The man is happiest who lives from day to day and asks
no more, garnering the simple goodness of a life.
~ Euripides

The Fullness of Time

For the administration of the days of ful-
fillment—to bring everything together in
the Messiah, both things in heaven and
things on earth in Him. ~ Ephesians 1:10

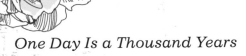

One Day Is a Thousand Years

Dear friends, don't let this one thing
escape you: With the Lord one day is
like a thousand years, and a thousand
years like one day. ~ 2 Peter 3:8

We turn not older with years, but newer every day.
~ Emily Dickinson

The Glory to Come

For I consider that the sufferings of this
present time are not worth compar-
ing with the glory that is going to be
revealed to us. ~ Romans 8:18

Delight in the Lord

I delight to do Your will, my God; Your
instruction lives within me." ~ Psalm 40:8

Receive every day as a resurrection from death, as a
new enjoyment of life. ~ William Law

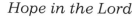

Hope in the Lord

Happy is the one whose help is the God of Jacob, whose hope is in the LORD his God. ~ Psalm 146:5

Change your thoughts and you change your world.
~ Norman Vincent Peale

Trust in the Lord

Trust in the LORD with all your heart, and do not rely on your own understanding; think about Him in all your ways, and He will guide you on the right paths. ~ Proverbs 3:5–6

Think about These Things

Finally brothers, whatever is true, whatever is honorable, whatever is just, whatever is pure, whatever is lovely, whatever is commendable—if there is any moral excellence and if there is any praise—dwell on these things. ~ Philippians 4:8

All our talents increase in the using,
and every faculty, both good and bad, strengthens
by exercise. ~ Anne Bronte

Be Transformed in Your Mind

> Do not be conformed to this age, but
> be transformed by the renewing of your
> mind, so that you may discern what is the
> good, pleasing, and perfect will of God.
> ~ Romans 12:2

Prayer

Lord, as I wake up fully to this day, let me
embrace the moments and all that You have for me.
Let me savor the opportunities to open the hearts and
minds of my students and reveal Your direction for
all of our lives. Amen.

Chapter 10

BUILD THE FUTURE

Perhaps the most difficult part of a teacher's job is anticipating, preparing, and equipping students for the future. The "future" keeps changing dramatically as the impact of new technologies and the effect of new cures for diseases is measured. Preparing for an uncertain future in a world built on mistrust and fear, cultivating a heart for God in an environment that questions His very existence, is a monumental task.

Yet, here you are. God has called you to be His voice and to shape His people for the years ahead. The best part is that He has not left you alone in that task. He has given you resources and other members of the faith community to help you along the way. He has given you His own Son to guide your steps. Some days, you may be called upon to face your own fears, to work through frustrating situations, or to keep walking even when the way is uncertain. All of that comes with building a future.

The good news is that God promises to always be with you and that nothing is impossible with Him. Those promises have stood the test of time and are in effect no matter how many other things change in the world.

You can help your students build the future because you have God's help. May He bless you abundantly today.

The Bible Promises . . .

When You're Afraid

> The LORD is my light and my salvation—whom should I fear? The LORD is the stronghold of my life—of whom should I be afraid? When evildoers came against me to devour my flesh, my foes and my enemies stumbled and fell. Though an army deploys against me, my heart is not afraid; though a war breaks out against me, still I am confident. ~ Psalm 27:1–3

*In God alone is there faithfulness and faith in the trust
that we may hold to him, to his promise, and to his
guidance. To hold to God is to rely on the fact that God
is there for me, and to live in this certainty.
~ Karl Barth*

Perfect Love

There is no fear in love; instead, perfect love drives out fear, because fear involves punishment. So the one who fears has not reached perfection in love. ~ 1 John 4:18

You're the Clay

I am disgusted with my life. I will express my complaint and speak in the bitterness of my soul. I will say to God: "Do not declare me guilty! Let me know why You prosecute me. Is it good for You to oppress, to reject the work of Your hands, and favor the plans of the wicked?

"Do You have eyes of flesh, or do You see as a human sees? Are Your days like those of a human, or Your years like those of a man, that You look for my wrongdoing and search for my sin, even though You know that I am not wicked and that there is no one who can deliver from Your hand?

"Your hands shaped me and formed me. Will You now turn and destroy me? Please remember that You formed me like clay. Will You now return me to dust?" ~ Job 10:1–9

It is not your business to succeed, but to do right; when you have done so, the rest lies with God. ~ C. S. Lewis

---

When You're Exhausted

Be gracious to me, LORD, for I am weak; heal me, LORD, for my bones are shaking; my whole being is shaken with terror. And You, LORD—how long? ~ Psalm 6:2–3

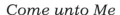

Come unto Me

"Come to Me, all of you who are weary
and burdened, and I will give you rest.
All of you, take up My yoke and learn
from Me, because I am gentle and
humble in heart, and you will find rest
for yourselves. For My yoke is easy and
My burden is light." ~ Matthew 11:28–30

When You're Worried

"This is why I tell you: Don't worry
about your life, what you will eat or what
you will drink; or about your body, what
you will wear. Isn't life more than food
and the body more than clothing? Look
at the birds of the sky: They don't sow
or reap or gather into barns, yet your
heavenly Father feeds them. Aren't you
worth more than they? Can any of you
add a single cubit to his height by worrying? And why do you worry about
clothes? Learn how the wildflowers
of the field grow: they don't labor or
spin thread. Yet I tell you that not even
Solomon in all his splendor was adorned
like one of these! If that's how God

clothes the grass of the field, which is here today and thrown into the furnace tomorrow, won't He do much more for you—you of little faith? So don't worry, saying, 'What will we eat?' or 'What will we drink?' or 'What will we wear?' For the idolaters eagerly seek all these things, and your heavenly Father knows that you need them. But seek first the kingdom of God and His righteousness, and all these things will be provided for you. Therefore don't worry about tomorrow, because tomorrow will worry about itself. Each day has enough trouble of its own." ~ Matthew 6:25–34

Whatever sort of tribulation we suffer, we should always remember that its purpose is to make us spurn the present and reach out to the future. ~ John Calvin

---

Commit Your Way to the Lord

Commit your activities to the LORD, and your plans will be achieved. ~ Proverbs 16:3

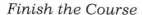

Finish the Course

> But I count my life of no value to myself, so that I may finish my course and the ministry I received from the Lord Jesus, to testify to the gospel of God's grace. ~ Acts 20:24

The God of Hope

> Now may the God of hope fill you with all joy and peace as you believe in Him so that you may overflow with hope by the power of the Holy Spirit. ~ Romans 15:13

God Is Your Shield

> Better a day in Your courts than a thousand anywhere else. I would rather be at the door of the house of my God than to live in the tents of wicked people. For the LORD God is a sun and shield. The LORD gives grace and glory; He does not withhold the good from those who live with integrity. Happy is the person who trusts in You, LORD of Hosts! ~ Psalm 84:10–12

Renewed Each Day

Indeed, everything is for your benefit, so that grace, extended through more and more people, may cause thanksgiving to increase to God's glory.

Therefore we do not give up. Even though our outer person is being destroyed, our inner person is being renewed day by day. For our momentary light affliction is producing for us an absolutely incomparable eternal weight of glory. So we do not focus on what is seen, but on what is unseen. For what is seen is temporary, but what is unseen is eternal. ~ 2 Corinthians 4:15–18

Run to Obtain the Prize

Don't you know that the runners in a stadium all race, but only one receives the prize? Run in such a way to win the prize. Now everyone who competes exercises self-control in everything. However, they do it to receive a crown that will fade away, but we a crown that will never fade away. Therefore I do not run like one who runs aimlessly or box like one beating the air. Instead, I discipline my body and bring it under strict control, so that after preaching to others, I myself will not be disqualified. ~ 1 Corinthians 9:24–27

Follow Me

Then Jesus said to His disciples, "If anyone wants to come with Me, he must deny himself, take up his cross, and follow Me. For whoever wants to save his life will lose it, but whoever loses his life because of Me will find it. What will it benefit a man if he gains the whole world yet loses his life? Or what will a man give in exchange for his life?" ~ Matthew 16:24–26

Live in Grace

For the grace of God has appeared with salvation for all people, instructing us to deny godlessness and worldly lusts and to live in a sensible, righteous, and godly way in the present age. ~ Titus 2:11–12

Speak Truth

These are the things you must do: Speak truth to one another; make true and sound decisions within your gates.
~ Zechariah 8:16

God's Plans for You

"For I know the plans I have for you"—this is the Lord's declaration—"plans for your welfare, not for disaster, to give you a future and a hope." ~ Jeremiah 29:11

Walk by Faith

For we know that if our temporary, earthly dwelling is destroyed, we have a building from God, an eternal dwelling in the heavens, not made with hands. Indeed, we groan in this body, desiring to put on our dwelling from heaven, since, when we are clothed, we will not be found naked. Indeed, we groan while we are in this tent, burdened as we are, because we do not want to be unclothed but clothed, so that mortality may be swallowed up by life. And the One who prepared us for this very purpose is God, who gave us the Spirit as a down payment.

So, we are always confident and know that while we are at home in the body we are away from the Lord. For we walk by faith, not by sight, and we are confident and satisfied to be out of the body and at home with the Lord.
~ 2 Corinthians 5:1–8

What you can do, or dream you can, begin it.
Boldness has genius, power and magic in it.
Only engage, and then the mind grows heated;
Begin it and the task will be completed. ~ Goethe

Diligence

The one who works his land will have plenty of food, but whoever chases fantasies lacks sense.

The diligent hand will rule, but laziness will lead to forced labor.

Anxiety in a man's heart weighs it down, but a good word cheers it up.

A righteous man is careful in dealing with his neighbor, but the ways of the wicked lead them astray.

A lazy man doesn't roast his game, but to a diligent man, his wealth is precious. ~ Proverbs 12:11, 24–27

Well done is better than well said.
~ Benjamin Franklin

To Whom Much Is Given

But the one who did not know and did things deserving of blows will be beaten lightly. Much will be required of everyone who has been given much. And even more will be expected of the one who has been entrusted with more. ~ Luke 12:48

That person is a success who has lived well, laughed often and loved much; who has gained the respect of intelligent people and the love of children; who has filled a niche and accomplished a task; who leaves the world better than how it was found, whether by an improved poppy, a perfect poem or a rescued soul; who never lacked appreciation of earth's beauty or failed to express it; who looked for the best in others and gave the best in return. ~ *Robert Louis Stevenson (adapted)*

Joy Comes

I will exalt You, Lord, because You have lifted me up and have not allowed my enemies to triumph over me. Lord my God, I cried to You for help, and You healed me. Lord, You brought me up from Sheol; You spared me from among those going down to the Pit.

Sing to Yahweh, you His faithful ones, and praise His holy name. For His anger lasts only a moment, but His favor, a lifetime. Weeping may spend the night, but there is joy in the morning.
~ Psalm 30:1–5

Strength to Strength

Happy are the people whose strength is in You, whose hearts are set on pilgrimage. As they pass through the Valley of Baca, they make it a source of springwater; even the autumn rain will cover it with blessings. They go from strength to strength; each appears before God in Zion. ~ Psalm 84:5–7

Commit Your Way to the Lord

Commit your activities to the LORD, and your plans will be achieved. ~ Proverbs 16:3

The great thing is to be found at one's post as a child of God, living each day as though it were our last, but planning as though our world might last a hundred years. ~ C. S. Lewis

---

God's Servants

And do not offer any parts of it to sin as weapons for unrighteousness. But as those who are alive from the dead, offer yourselves to God, and all the parts of yourselves to God as weapons for righteousness. For sin will not rule over you, because you are not under law but under grace.

What then? Should we sin because we are not under law but under grace? Absolutely not! Don't you know that if you offer yourselves to someone as obedient slaves, you are slaves of that one you obey—either of sin leading to death or of obedience leading to righteousness? But thank God that, although you used to be slaves of sin, you obeyed from the heart that pattern of teaching you were transferred to, and having been liberated from sin, you became enslaved to righteousness. ~ Romans 6:13–18

Jesus Has Gone Ahead of You

"Your heart must not be troubled. Believe in God; believe also in Me. In My Father's house are many dwelling places; if not, I would have told you. I am going away to prepare a place for you. If I go away and prepare a place for you, I will come back and receive you to Myself, so that where I am you may be also. You know the way to where I am going."

"Lord," Thomas said, "we don't know where You're going. How can we know the way?"

Jesus told him, "I am the way, the truth, and the life. No one comes to the Father except through Me." ~ John 14:1–6

Never be afraid to trust an unknown future to a known God. ~ Corrie Ten Boom

---

Blessed Work

Then I heard a voice from heaven saying, "Write: The dead who die in the Lord from now on are blessed."

"Yes," says the Spirit, "let them rest from their labors, for their works follow them!" ~ Revelation 14:13

A New Earth

Then I saw a new heaven and a new earth, for the first heaven and the first earth had passed away, and the sea no longer existed. I also saw the Holy City,

new Jerusalem, coming down out of
heaven from God, prepared like a bride
adorned for her husband.

Then I heard a loud voice from the
throne: Look! God's dwelling is with
humanity, and He will live with them.
They will be His people, and God Himself will be with them and be their God.
~ Revelation 21:1–3

---

*Even if I knew that tomorrow the world
would go to pieces, I would still plant my apple tree.*
~ Martin Luther

Prayer

Dear Lord,
*Only You hold the future. You know what
You want from my each day and what plans You
have. Direct my steps and help me to continue to
serve You and my students in ways that bring the
greatest possibilities. Thank You for Your stead-
fast promises. Amen.*

Notes

_____

_____

_____

_____

_____

_____

_____

_____

_____

_____

_____

_____

Notes

_____

_____

_____

_____

_____

_____

_____

_____

_____

_____

_____

_____

_____